P9-CFQ-615

Also by Meredith Holmes

Shubad's Crown

FAMILIAR
AT
FIRST
THEN
STRANGE

FAMILIAR AT FIRST THEN STRANGE

MEREDITH HOLMES

POND ROAD PRESS
WASHINGTON, DC
NORTH TRURO, MA

Copyright © 2015 by Meredith Holmes.
All rights reserved.
Printed in the United States of America.

Cover art: Special thanks go to the Provincetown Art
Association and Museum (PAAM) in Provincetown,
MA, for permission to use, as a courtesy, Joan Pereira's
painting, "Kafka's Village at Dawn" (oil on canvas).
Special thanks go to the artist Joan Pereira for her
copyright permission as a courtesy.

Cover art photograph: James Zimmerman, PAAM.

Book design and layout: Mary Ann Larkin and
Patric Pepper.

ISBN: 978-0-9719741-6-6
Library of Congress Control Number: 2015943463

Further acknowledgments follow page 56.

Pond Road Press
Mary Ann Larkin and Patric Pepper
221 Channing Street NE
Washington, DC 20002
pepperlarkin@juno.com

Available through Amazon.com and other online
booksellers, and through Pond Road Press.

for Loretta, for everything

Contents

Familiar
at
First
Then
Strange

Obeying Rilke, I Have Seen Many Cities

I have seen the bravado of Munich
its fresh-faced cyclists
the reconstructed pilasters and rosettes
the prosperous widows refusing
the Museum of Degenerate Art.
The marbled sanctuary of Lima's cafes,
the millions clinging to her voluminous
skirts, washing sheets in drainage ditches.
Boston, where erudition rumbles
from hill to hill, the capitol dome glitters,
and people ride swans on the river.
Quaker Philadelphia, bathed in distillery
offal and cold Atlantic mist, Elfreth's
Alley hidden at its whorled center.
But none of these cities, not even Paris
with its exquisite moodiness
and a makeover more mesmerizing
than Maria Callas's, matches the city
of my exile. Nothing compares
with the windows I gaze through there,
hair uncombed, coffee cup in hand.
No encounters are more wrenching
than chance meetings on those
narrow streets, first snow falling.
There is no light more melancholy
than the afternoon light of this city
and none boasts entrances
as stately, exits more graceful.

How You'll Recognize Me

I'll wait by the door.
I'll be wearing a long black
coat and grey mittens.
I'll have brown hair—
medium brown, medium long.
I'll be the medium girl
with a notebook and a pen.
I'll be the skinny girl
in cut-off jeans and glasses.
I'll be the wallflower
waiting by the door,
the girl in a white
sleeveless blouse
to whom nothing
is going to happen.
I'll be empty-handed
except for the notebook.
I'll be the one who did it
on the bleachers
and on a bed of moss
and under the old apple tree.
I'll be waiting by the door
and I'll have auburn hair
and bird-and-star earrings
I found in a thrift store.
I'll be holding a small
child by the hand
and I'll look as if I've seen a ghost.
I'll be so bundled up
in my long black coat
you won't recognize me.
I'll be carrying a notebook
and I'll be waiting by the door.

My Double Life

The summer we were ten, Lizzie and I
went barefoot all day, played Spit, guzzled
Coke, and compared vaccination scars.
We denied liking school, teased
her little sister, and stole small
change from my brother's dresser.
But I really lived in another world
in which I felt the trees sigh with pleasure
when it rained, and grieved as for an old uncle
when the maple lost a limb in a thunderstorm.
I read the day, felt its forehead for fever
and watched from the doorway
if it seemed restless.
I was alert to the crosstalk of jays
and hand mowers, the constant
confetti of songbirds and cicadas,
and I could not forget how once
a wasp caught its feet in the screen
and how the tone and timbre
of everything flowed through me.

Summer Reading

On the shady porch of our rented cottage
I devour ten library books in three days.
Locusts harmonize in the tulip trees,
sunlight and bees pour from unmown fields,
and I ransack the cottage for something to read.
I browse orphan volumes of the 1953 *World Book*,
body surf a blue biography of Luther
Burbank, daisy pioneer, and find and finish
by yellow bug light three Cherry Ames mysteries,
despised by my mother, who is silent
for now, on the subject of "potboilers."
When she draws water for coffee,
the kitchen pump moans—metal clashing
on metal—and for a few seconds, nothing
happens, then a torrent of cold, clean
water, smelling of earth and stone,
leaps up the pump's throat and out
into the white enamel saucepan
my mother holds in her left hand.
I dig through magazine racks and end tables
finding only limp back issues of *Boys' Life*,
TV Guide, and *Field & Stream*.
Several times, I open my mother's
copy of *Doctor Zhivago*, but do not
feel equal even to the book flap.
Near the end of our two-week stay
I discover, in the attic crawl space,
a stash of comic books, and for days,
sawdust furring my sweaty skin,
I wander the flat, fevered worlds
of Green Lantern, Supergirl,
and Betty & Veronica.

The Volcano

My caldera is open to the sky and its daily rainstorms.
The entrance to the interior blocked by a forest
so mature, medicinal plants are hunted
in the understory, and humans zipline the canopy
ecstatically imitating their living ancestors.
Acacia, breadfruit, and Cook pine flow up
the inside of my cone, and I am bored to death
with this extinction, this stiffness in the mantle.
I prefer the term "dormant" and wait
for a thunderous shift, for stinging ash
and flames and snakes of lava
to hiss through the trees, devouring
the lush accumulation of decades.

Time and Matter in Hayden Hall

My advisor means well.
He asks me about my future:
What do you intend to do with your life?
Are you planning to teach?
"Intend." "Life." I turn these words
over in my mind, but understand nothing.
They are smooth, mute artifacts,
which I hand back without comment.

Weighed down by immediate sensations,
I live on an enormous planet,
where gravity is 100 times stronger
than on Earth, and one day lasts for weeks.
If you worked on your thesis a little bit
every day, my advisor explains patiently,
you could finish by the deadline.
I grasp the power of the incremental
but not as it applies to me.

My advisor's wool jacket hangs
on its hook like the Pleistocene.
Above us, the dust of dispersed
galaxies drifts across the afternoon.
On the desk lies the written record
of my checkered academic career.
I am made of atoms from which
the property of urgency is absent.
My only motion is backward
from stillness through paralysis
to a solid state, indistinguishable
(without extremely sensitive
equipment) from nothingness.

Three Snapshots

1.
Here I am in the back yard
the August before I turned three.
The day I had my first thought.
The thought was, *this is me*
this is me, this is me thinking
it's hot, this is me thinking.
The thought ricocheted
around the cage of my skull
with swelling clarity
coiling and tightening its grip.
Then I stood in blazing
sunlight by the garage door
which sagged open
and revealed a wedge
of cool, dirt-floor darkness.
This was a relief to see
and the hydrangea's blue
and the sweet, white
corridors of clean sheets
hanging on the line.

2.
This was taken sometime
during the decade
in which I did not exist.
I rarely saw friends or family,
wrote nothing, said little.
See how I'm standing apart
from my father there
as if we were estranged?
It began with her saying,
"You're so easy
to get along with."
The next thing was,

"We need to sell your desk."
And finally, "You say *we* too much."
I scanned every thought
before I spoke, checking
for possible trouble.
The effect was corrosive
first changing the color
and texture of the surface
then eating deeper, weakening
the whole structure, pulling
bolts loose and spitting them
onto the waste ground below.

3.
Much later, a new century
a second life, and the family reunion.
You were four; I was forty-five.
The last thing I wanted to do
that day was go swimming.
It was early May, chilly and cloudy,
trees a tender celery green
leaves still tightly furled.
But you'd been waiting all day
to get in the pool, so I jumped in
first and held out my arms
while you got ready, knees bent,
toes gripping the hard
blue edge, arms straight back—
wings for skipping into thin air.
You said you weren't cold
and you clasped me fiercely
with your arms and chubby knees,
your whole soaking, shivering
self, wanting this consummation,
this shrieking village of splashing,
diving, and breaching to last forever.

Horoscope

You will endure an interval of diminishing returns
a time of ebb with no flow, a long season of waning.
Everything, especially money and invitations to the beach,
will fall through your fingers like water onto thirsty sand.
If someone asks you out to a movie, you will cough
all through it, then spend the weekend in bed.
On Monday, you will feel well enough to go to work.
Free time will become the object of romantic love,
the source of your greatest pleasure and sharpest pain.
The graceful, sunlit corridors of Saturday mornings
will be, by noon, cluttered with plumbing estimates
and personal accounts that refuse to be reconciled.
You will be on hold with the insurance company
for the entire summer pageant. You will miss stilt walkers
in peacock feathers and gifted children pirouetting
into the crowd, giving away real red roses.
Your best friends will move to cities with more sun
and bustle, better jobs, and fountains downtown.
They will never think twice about doing this.

Full Moon

The moonlight poured down and rippled
like white silk
between the houses across the street.
I noticed this
as I shoved the last bookcase into the U-Haul
on the coldest night of the year.
The moonlight slid around oaks and maples
that were creaking like ships at anchor
and pooled exactly where I stood in the street.
Then the moonlight spoke
in a calm, clear voice:
Don't go back inside.
Run, run for your life.

Four Minds I Know

1.

She ploughs fields both over-farmed and fallow
then takes to the air to see the patchwork
of ellipses and parabolas, strict form, free verse.
Piloting her own noisy biplane, she writes the big
questions, white on blue, in swooping exhaust.
Back on the ground the threshing never ceases.
She beats the grain and flings it skyward, reading
the messages written there, gold on blue.
These, by her lights, are just more questions.
Mind is idiosyncratic as fingerprint or iris.

2.

Dubbed the family beauty, she was summa cum
laude, with a rare species of copper-colored hair.
Strong pinions, fresh plumage, and sturdy DNA
took her far, and the soaring seemed effortless
until she collided with an obdurate, invisible thing.
Then a long dive, wings folded tight as a cormorant's
and a heavy afterlife of uphill climbs, basement
apartments, and the daily defense of sanity.
But gravity made her tough, and her head is hard.
She contrives to outwit confinement of all kinds.

3.

Unangelically, he enlists his heart to mentor his mind.
Homeschooled, and in need of discipline, he learns
to listen and wait, and to confront the freshets
of grief flowing through certain, bypassed places.
Unbored and unafraid, his mind balances
on a wire strung not far above the ground

between two young, straight trees. It breathes
the good clean air and aromatic earth
then sets out on its wobbly, dangerous walk
muscular and big-hearted as a breezing horse.

4.
"She's intelligent, but . . ." I hear my teacher say
just before the infirmary door clicks shut.
The cot is narrow, the green wool blanket rough
and I have a migraine triggered by long division.
The District has just released a secret number:
my intelligence quotient, which I may not know
but which my mother hints is only average.
I begin to understand how the intelligence business
hinges on strategic silences and endorsed disinformation.
Despite intelligence withheld, mind finds a way.

Old Flame

Thirty-six years have passed
and I get jealous just reading a poem
about a man who might be you.
One of your exes is visiting—
it's her poem—and patience is required
on her part; you are restrained
and sad. It could easily be you.
An island in Maine, an old
Chevy pickup, raspberries,
blackberries, and blueberries
ripening at the same time
all of us wading into the woods
with buckets, bowls, and jars,
anything we could fill.
The man in the poem likes cats
which, as I recall, you did.
And he's been married five times.
There would have been time for that.
Now you and this ex-wife
or girlfriend are walking together
through the hemlocks
on the north side of the island
and she is taking everything in:
the narrow path down to the water
the apple-green garter snake
looping suddenly out of the tall grass
the rowboat you use for trips to town.
Now I remember how it was:
me unfolding like a one-page letter
you touching a match to one corner
all the words burning away, everything
turning to the thinnest, lightest ash.

Devolving: A Dream

This can't be.
I learned to walk on land,
a long process, but orderly:
speck, gill, mouth, legs.
Now I am unlearning it all
just when something is chasing me.
I'm sinking to my knees
loping on all fours up a grassy knoll
my back legs too long, front legs too short.
I'm no match for my pursuer
who is pulling me backwards into its jaws.
I am lemur, sloth, mouse, creature
of leaf litter and worm-tilled earth,
salamander, slug.
It can't be true.
It has always been true.

Turning Sixty

after Katha Pollitt's "Turning Thirty"

Such were the immediate preoccupations—
your daughter sawing the umbilical
with an old, dull knife, your mother's
ghost rattling the silverware and the good
dishes, your siblings obeying the rules
of atmospheric perspective and disappearing
into the out-of-state distance—
that your sixtieth birthday passed without notice.

Everybody says you look younger
than you are, and you go along,
for once believing wholeheartedly
in a truth that's only skin-deep.
You color your hair, a deception
unthinkable to your 20-something self.

You think you've set aside the spooling
third-person narrative that places you
at the center of a subtle and strangely
affecting novel about your life so far.
But you notice there's a car vibrating
in the driveway, the doorbell is ringing
and you aren't ready.

Your high school friends make jokes
about being old that you don't think
are funny, because they have aged
shockingly, laughing with creased
crumpled faces, and because you
got such a late start on everything.
You have only now grabbed the bridle
of the shy, fickle horse you recognize
as your own life.

Dreaming My Life

A grey dream, and persistent:
Walking into a chilly wind
unable to stop thinking,
This is me walking into a chilly wind.
I feel horizontal, like lines on a page,
and odd things break my heart:
a woman with an enormous Gallic nose
slowly, thoughtfully walking uphill,
yellow bulldozers seeming to destroy
a field in time to Handel's *Water Music.*
It might be my birthday in this dream,
and when it is, a long table blazes white.
All around it hands and faces are lit.
Behind them—darkness.
A northern city, massive
nineteenth-century buildings,
an early November evening,
streets slicked with rain.
Someone might love me.
I open my umbrella and hurry
over the shining surfaces.
Behind me—colonnades of decades,
a continent of melancholy.

My Five Favorite Things of Last Year

1.
That blue and silver night.
Frost, stars, and a self-possessed sky
singing so beautifully, so inaudibly
we all wondered where
we'd heard the song before.

2.
Rediscovering the earth in March.
Kissed it with my feet.
Miles and miles of hoofing it from the hip.
Time passed, or I passed it—couldn't tell.
Trees, sky, dogs, and people on porches
shot by like stage scenery on rails.
I wasn't careful, and I didn't care.

3.
Time stopped, and cherry trees
in full bloom stood perfectly still.
We kept moving, of course, circling
the pink and white clouds.
I can't think of a single person
who took the trees for granted.
City officials disabled the street lamps
and we walked after dark
in cherry blossom light.

4.
The fox in Lake View Cemetery.
I stop the car to get a good look at him.
He trots head down, eying me sideways.
He is so beautiful with his black paws

and narrow face, so canine and feline.
You are so beautiful! I say inside my car.
You're so beautiful! That's all Dick Cavett,
tongue-tied for once, could say
to foxy Diana Rigg, when she finally
consented to curl up on his TV studio couch.
She looked both pleased and wary
with her gorgeous plume of a tail
wrapped around her ankles.
But my fox's foxiness came first.

5.
Our conversations.
People like you are extremely rare.
You listen with a light in your eyes
others call "intelligence,"
but which I experience
as spaciousness, an end to impasse.
High clouds and a lifting wind
when we talk at the kitchen table
your head tilted, chin in hand.

Injunction for a Slow Fall

Just wait, please.
Stop to stare into the seedy soul
of a late tomato.
Pause to rip the green bodices
of sweet corn, and do not neglect
to applaud the crickets,
fewer and fainter every night,
one by one, bowing offstage
exquisite, irreplaceable instruments
tucked under their arms.

Les Nympheas at the Orangerie

We are only minor deities,
but so beautiful that thousands
troop through these plain
ovular rooms just to look at us.
Even the most cloddish
stop breathing for a few seconds
but they can't bear it for long
so they talk to each other
or glance down at their maps
and wander into the next room.

It is our task only to be, and by being
incandescently, immortally lovely
bind humans to the trees and rivers.
People have speech—principally naming—
which does not satisfy, but comforts them.
Young girls notice how we bathe all
in a beautifying amniotic mist
(even their itchy little brothers
and the guard on his metal chair)
so they bask on the gallery benches
hoping something of us
will soak through their skin.

Humans have one other consolation,
and we were reminded of it today
when a sensible, white-haired woman
entered the gallery, saw us for the first time,
and burst into tears.

Nina

When I lived in French
she sometimes says, or, *Oh*
I was so young and Italian then.
I hardly know myself in English,
but I've rediscovered Rilke,
and he's led me home to German.
Alone in her study
Nina peers at a word.
She sees things we don't:
Latin roots, Germanic stalk
French flowers, and the little
stones paths leading
from one word to the next.
She travels these, studying
the kitchens and workshops
of language, the belts and gears
and coal fires, people busy doing
the tangible: wrighting wheels,
tanning hides, setting type.
Nina grasps her pen,
listening and remembering.

Second Language

I admired her fluency.
She could dance, slam doors,
and mutter in Spanish,
and when called upon to do so,
admire babies, grand pianos, and caged birds.
She was at ease on the street
having mastered several dialects
including moneychanger and child beggar.
She was also agile in formal situations
such as widowed matriarch,
candle-lit supper with host's mistress,
power outage, and impending coup.
What I envied most was how she got jokes
and even made them, her remarkable
facility with Spanish laughter.

Jeanne

She loved, was wooed by,
and eventually married Paris.
She abandoned Los Angeles,
the lout, for Paris and its *allées*
and insularity, its North Africans
and fountains frequented by tousled
muscled Greek gods, its *quartier
juif*, its *orangeries* and *bureaucracies*,
the many subtle dialects of which,
being bright, she quickly mastered.
She learned to flirt in the 19th,
bought an apartment there, and spent
a fortune on a washing machine.
She had an Arab boyfriend
and an African boyfriend
and always a plan B.
She cooked rarely, changed
her first name and reclaimed her last.
She wrote a guidebook and mapped
the best Belgian chocolate boutiques.
Her photos still hang in Yusef's cafe.
She traveled Paris by train, on foot,
by bus and barge; her thousand
circuits, a gold ring, well-fingered.

September

She's a bit blowsy
but still beautiful,
and in a certain light,
blooming at her peak—
asters, peaches, and tides
of flowering vines foaming
over walls and fences.
She's thinner now, her fields
of wild grass drier, sparser.
Subtle, elliptical, her leaves
crinkling at the corners,
she never alludes
to the sadness underneath it all
as she walks us to the equinox
in her long, breezy dress.

Field Notes: Church Service

Against my better judgment, I go to church with Agnes.
She means to ask Jesus for help on our behalf.
I have never understood importuning Jesus
and am so embarrassed, I hope he's hard of hearing.
Equally baffling: when the preacher raises his right
forefinger, congregants riffle their Bibles.
What are they looking for?
The sermon: recognizing angels at the airport.
I pray (in my way) for a wrestling match
in the choir loft, with robes ripped and toupees tossed.
Nothing happens, except when cookies and coffee
in the narthex are announced, there is a deep
wooden groan, as pews release their burdens
a rustling of feathers as congregants regain speech.

The Gardener

She staked her claim in December, occupying
the abandoned lot with a hill of topsoil
and a wheelbarrow full of stones.
In March, a thaw, more snow and waiting.
Then one morning, a circle of turned earth
and a week later, two lanterns swinging
on low branches of the hawthorn
and paths edged with broken crockery.
In the rising tide of daylight, snow drops
and wind chimes shivering in the dogwood.
By June, hydrangeas blooming along the fence,
a kitchen chair painted eggplant, and pole beans
trained up a wigwam of old rake handles.
All summer there are lights in the trees.
The gardener resists autumn until late November
and even then, her dahlias are huge and bright.
She waves to me from a park bench
she dragged down the street in September.
A black dog, her familiar, sits bolt upright
beside her in the softly falling snow.
They exchange a few words.
She sips thoughtfully from a blue mug
and watches her garden give in to the cold.

Clearing Out

When Elwood's widow, Mildred
finally felt up to it, she asked us
to clear out his workshop:
"Everything goes, but leave me
a decent hammer and a pair of pliers."
It was a beautiful morning:
blue sky, blue hydrangeas
and the Chesapeake, which
you can see from Mildred's
front yard, was blue and quiet.
We entered Elwood's shop
in a mood of reverence.
It was cool in there and still
smelled like kerosene.
First, we carried out the Evinrudes
(there were three) and laid each one
in a nest of old blankets.
Then two table saws and a generator,
a spool of nautical rope,
two power mowers, a sump pump
and a porcelain toilet with all the parts.
Ed took the fishing gear.
I found some old hand tools:
a plane, a level, and a miter box.
I asked Mildred did she mind.
She waved her hands
in the direction of the bay:
"Just get it out of here."
We counted five toolboxes
and three sets of socket wrenches.
"On second thought," said Mildred

"leave me the gardening tools."
I filled two wooden crates
and a coal scuttle with nails, all sizes,
and poured the rest in a grocery bag.
We were just going, when I noticed
a perfect snakeskin
coiled by the foundation.
I wanted it for my little girl
but when I touched it
the whole thing turned to powder
and I had to leave it where it was.

Friends Like These

1.
Our reunion is a far cry
from what I'd imagined.
First, you announce
you can't stay long
and in the little time we have
you concentrate on my failure
to get a driver's license.
What about my pristine
credit rating, my nine to five
and my very adult grasp
of train and bus schedules?
I'd planned on us sitting around
my refinished Goodwill table.
I'd introduce my cobbled-together
family, and we'd talk about
all those years of making
something out of nothing.

2.
You say you should be writing
your stories, which at first poured
effortlessly onto the page like stars
with their ancient light intact.
But tonight you don't
feel like writing.
No, No! I want to scream
Don't be like me!

3.
I loved your tale of trying to ride two
bikes at once, western-stagecoach style

when you were nine, because that's exactly
when I was riding my green bike
all over town and roller-skating
at the railroad equipment depot.
Think of it! Me in New Jersey, you
in North Carolina, doing the same things!
When I heard rain, you heard it, too
and we ran outside to taste and smell it
and feel it Niagara down on us.

4.
The one who dreamed
the same dreams as foxes
and reminted herself silver
the one who loved forget-me-not
blue above all other blues
the one whose absence
convinced us the earth is flat
the one who was ground
as beach glass, to translucence
that one is gone.

Why I Want To Be on the Softball Team, Even Though I Can't Hit or Catch

Games two times a week
on the field by the lake.
I'd be out in left field,
of course, hands on my thighs
waiting, always ready for a fly
ball, high and outside, or a line drive.
Just past first base would be Lake Erie
fragrant in spite of everything
and restless, plotting her next move,
but right now, just enjoying the game.
We'd all cram into the dugout,
the bench not quite long enough
for all of us, and me, thoughtfully
punching my glove, while nighthawks
spill from the trees and skim the infield.
We'd play the day right down
to the smooth, blue horizon.
Afterward, covered in dust and good
sweat, gloves folded, we'd walk slowly
back to our cars, together, a team
in summer, on the lake.

I Remember You

as you were in the middle of the night
when I couldn't sleep, not afraid of the dark—
just bored by it, because you seemed indifferent then
your street lights droning, and my father
across the hall, snoring like an idling truck.
Sometimes your dogs (they were all mutts then)
howled just before the metallic baying
of your sirens filled the air, and John McRory
the volunteer fireman next door, slammed
into his station wagon and roared off to save you.

I remember you in the rain
how you surrendered to it
giving up all your secrets
how we ran on ahead, sheltered at first
by your lindens and locusts
then the rain plunging straight down
melting our shirts and getting under our skin.
We tore through your short cuts,
rain-soaked grass taking prints of our feet.
We skidded onto your porches
panting, unscathed, and untransformed.

I remember you in November
the shapes of your oaks and maples revealed.
You were your trees somehow, and what a pleasure
to see those vaulted bones again.
We viewed skeletons dispassionately, noting
the slender, mobile twigs at the terminus
of each branch, how the limbs joined trunk
and the whole hinted at roots we could not see.

Class Photo

The origin of the universe was freshman math
class, when my father turned from the window
with its excellent view of the women's tennis courts
and noticed my mother. She tutored him in algebra
and without knowing how to skate, he leapt
barrels for her on the frozen reservoir.
They graduated, married, and found work.
My two brothers spun off like asteroids
all in a time before time began.

At their twentieth college reunion, I show up
in the front row of the class picture, smiling
a dolphin's smile, drifting in an amniotic sea.
My brothers shade their eyes with their hands.
Five year later, the class of 1929, trailing
children and spouses, spills downhill
behind the library to have its picture taken.
The campus steams—unusual for Boston
in June. My father drapes his suit jacket
over his arm. All the men wear white
shirts, and all the women, white gloves.
A bald man with a Brownie camera
holds it waist high, elbows out, like
a dowser and consults the bright
inverted image of the class of 1929.
"Closer," he yells, "move closer!"
We shuffle sideways to the center,
my parents link arms, my brothers
put their hands on my shoulders,
and we all squint into the sun.

American Sycamore

I was fostered by an American Sycamore
older, more majestic, and more vigorous
than all the oaks and maples in town.
The crown of our sycamore stretched
like a green tent over the house
and the roots drank from an ancient aquifer.

In April, the sycamore dropped thousands
of marble-sized buttonballs, hard, prickly
and tightly packed with pale seeds.
In August, like a prodigious snake
the sycamore shed rolls of bark
exposing new yellow skin.

My father and my brothers pitched
long ropes over the lowest limb
to make me a swing. I begged for run-unders,
planning to launch myself, at the peak
of my arc, into the unexplored green
regions of the sycamore's highest branches.

My mother read *Tale of Two Cities*
in a canvas chair under the sycamore.
"In Europe it's called a plane tree,"
she told me, looking up from the book
in her lap, bouquets of light and shadow
moving across her arms and shoulders.

"If anything happens to this tree
I don't want to live here anymore."

August

Aunts and uncles and cousins visiting
from Boston linger over breakfast
in a luxury of coffee, raisin toast,
and cigarette smoke. Outside the dining room
windows, the summer morning rustles
open and makes extravagant promises.
I am easy among the ashtrays
and the mystery magazines my aunt
purchased at the train station newsstand
for the annual trip down to New Jersey.
Unwashed, uncombed, and undetected,
I roam the guest rooms spying on the scuffed,
alien luggage, shaving kits, hairpins,
and watches colonizing the dressers.
I hide on the attic steps eating gold-wrapped
chocolate coins that John D. Mullaney
brings me every year, listening to family talk
roll through the house and up the stairs.
My father's voice is the deepest.
A big wave, it rises far offshore, moves
slowly, full of distant, indecipherable
music, and is the last to break on the sand.

Correspondence

My father and his brother wrote to each other for decades.
In New Jersey, on our side of the correspondence
the letters thundered into being on Sunday afternoons.
My father at the Royal manual, each hammered line
ending with a bell and helixing down to the next,
the whole sequence drawn together at the bottom
by his bold, upright signature. Then the envelope
and stamp and a short amble to the mailbox.
A week later—the answer from Boston
where both brothers were conceived.
The handwriting on the envelope resembled
my father's, but was more calligraphic, less active.
Fifty percent of siblings' genetic material is the same
but because of complex on-off switches in the DNA,
similarities may be few, subtle, or unexpressed.
My father—medium build, athletic, gregarious;
his older brother—tall, sedentary, silent.
My father smoked cigars, his brother, a pipe.
My father loved history, baseball, and old wood.
His brother loved trains, stained glass, poetry.
My father died of Alzheimer's; his brother, cancer.
My father's letters were not saved.
His brother's are boxed in a university archive,
while my father's half of the correspondence
has acquired the fluidity of memory,
his imagined imprint, a tinted transparency.

Ground Zero, 1955

My small hand enveloped
in my father's big cushiony one
I twitched and tapped down the bright
white aisle of washers and dryers at Sears
& Roebuck, in Camden, New Jersey.
When we stopped to inspect one,
my father told me to stand still.
I did stand still, and then I saw
that every third woman in the store
was pregnant. Women in maternity
smocks swarmed over mops and pails.
They stood in line to buy vacuum cleaners,
kitchenware, clothespins, and tableware.
They thumbed through the shirts and shoes,
underwear, pants, and socks.
I felt something speeding toward us,
gathering momentum, as when jets
flew over, racing the sound barrier,
and we clapped hands to ears,
waiting for the world-shattering boom.

The Memoirist Asks Where To Put the Story—Present or Past

Present, says the journalist.
It's intimate, intense, perfect
for your coming-to-terms tale
of harvesting grapes in France
with weather-hardened strangers
who crush fermented fruit
into the deep gash on your hand
which heals overnight.
The present is for bullets dodged
wild parties exited in tears minutes
before the house burns to the ground.
I speak from experience on a daily.
News moves fast.

You'd be happier in the past
says the poet, glancing at the forest
of oaks and beeches that once
surrounded the café where they sit.
She sees a faint, grassy track
winding through trees, just now
tumbling to October.
The past, she says.
That's where keys marry their locks
and stars, attentive as dancers
to a choreographer
take their true positions.

House Party

The Roosevelts lived with us for years
enjoying full use of the house.
Teddy liked a cigar, and my admiring
father never tired of hearing
about the charge up San Juan Hill.
Hardly an evening meal passed
without FDR, making my bigoted
grandfather apoplectic.
We loved Franklin for that.
Eleanor outstayed them all.
Her corsage always fresh
she gazed quietly at a darkening
world—so much still to be done—
and always gave my mother hope.

The Wizard of 213 Locust Street

for Chris on his 69th birthday

Grey-eyed, left-handed, mathematically gifted,
and right with statistically significant frequency,
my brother Chris was eight when I was born,
thirteen when I entered kindergarten.
He tricked me into riding my first two-wheeler,
showed me a system for alphabetizing spelling words,
and taught me how to tie my shoelaces.
Although I am right-handed
I still lace my shoes like a lefty.

Our mother railed against his messy room
the beat-up boxes full of junk,
the smelly socks, the unmade bed,
and the grass clippings he tracked in
from his lawn-mowing jobs.
So Chris paid me a dollar a week to clean
his room, and suddenly at age eight,
I was popsicle rich and stopped
stealing Chiclets and small change off his dresser.

First the floor: clothes in the closet, wet towels
on the rack, coke bottles in the wastebasket.
Then the bed: unload, make, reload.
I loved this glorious clutter, a codex
of his life I wanted to understand,
the layered archeology of an alien culture.
A baseball with a torn cover, plastic
ice cubes in which were embedded
real flies, a glass tube of litmus paper,

three *Pogo* books, a slide rule, some dice,
a framed portrait of Alfred E. Newman,
mechanical pencils, a Walden Pond ashtray
full of pennies, a nebbish holding an American flag,
a knee brace, and a paperback in German
with a wizard and a devil on the cover.
I wanted to know how the slide rule worked,
what litmus paper was, and why a college
freshman would read a book about magic.

Wisely, he did not try to explain the slide rule,
but demonstrated how litmus paper turned red
in an acid solution, blue in an alkaline.
We tested things we found around the house:
his aftershave and contact lens solution,
my iced tea with lemon, a dab of hot sauce.
The labile litmus seemed magic to me.
"This is chemistry, not alchemy,"
he told me, and I believed him.

He excelled at puzzles and brainteasers,
and loved to test guessing games on me.
"OK," he said pointing to the German book,
"I tell you some rules of German grammar,
you get one chance to pronounce the author's name.
All g's are hard; the first letter of a diphthong
is silent; t's are hard, and if a vowel
comes after a consonant, it's never silent."
I thought this over, and finally said, *Gurr-teh,*

October 1998

Our mother loosed the thick rope
from the pier, climbed down
into the dinghy, then drifted
close to shore for days.
Her struggle to catch a tail wind,
our long wait on hard kitchen chairs
was physical and intimate
like jamming your hip
against a stuck door
or lifting a child covered in mud
up and away from you.
It was real—the universe
swinging so low and close
we bent double, as under a pendulum.
It was both strange and ordinary
like our own voices
and the house of our childhood.
But there was nothing holy in it
only her last breath
and the mystery, not of the soul
but the body, how convincingly
it argued she was still there.

Letter to My Mother: Books, Christians, World Travel

I went to town hall last night
to hear Paul Theroux talk.
I expected the place to be packed
but only a few of the seats were filled.
Paul Theroux said people like us
who love books are like the early Christians
a small band who believe fiercely
in something impossible, against
which powerful forces are arrayed.
I thought you would have been
one of those early Christians.
You're that tough-minded.

Paul Theroux has stopped traveling.
He said there's nothing more
to be learned—not because
he knows it all, and not because
he sees a McDonald's in Venezuela
and Def Leopard t-shirts in Sri Lanka
but because evil has been franchised.
Everywhere he goes, there is a dictator
whose brother-in-law runs the secret police.
Schools and hospitals fall in tatters
and armies swell and shine.
Everywhere he goes, children's ribs
rise to the surface; the earth dries to powder
and takes to the air on a journey of its own.

Letter to My Mother: Julia Child

Tonight we watched Julia Child roast a chicken.
It's hard to imagine you tuning in to a cooking show
but you would have appreciated this one—
her uninhibited zest and her real affection
for the chicken, which she kept slapping
in a summer camp pal kind of way.
She brandished a fistful of parsley
(I know, your favorite herb!)
 while exhorting us to write our congressmen
if our state lacked strict chicken inspection laws.
Also in this episode, she advised us
to keep a toolbox right in the kitchen
in case we had to wrestle with an uncooperative
oven door or jammed roasting spit.
This reminded me of the time
you used a claw hammer to open
a tube of Pillsbury refrigerator rolls
when the instructions ("rap sharply
at 45 degree angle on table edge") didn't work.
I just think you would have liked the way
Julia Child took everything in hand:
chicken, parsley, U.S. Congress.

Letter to My Mother: Kieran

We're back from Frankfort.
I wish you could see Kieran.
He's five, now, your fourth great-grandson.
He has the complexion of an angel
and a naturalist's vocabulary.
Loquacious and thin-skinned,
Kieran likes to talk to cashiers
and security guards about their lives.
The other day his mother found him
in the cereal aisle of the PX, pressing
a marine for details about wildlife in Brazil:
"But what *kind* of golden tamarin?"
Kieran rarely smiles.
When he found out
what the Romans did to Jesus
he took it very hard.

Conversations with My Daughter

How am I doing?
Great. Fine. You're doing fine
but slow down.
It would be a good idea
to slow down at this intersection.

Is infinity an odd or an even number?
Neither. I think infinity
is an idea, not a number
but I'll check with a friend
who's good in math.

What does benevolent mean, again?
Kind. Good. A person who does no harm.
Oh. I think I would make a good dictator.
But this is a democracy.
Shush! I don't care.
I want absolute power over the Midwest.
I'd be benevolent. I'd invite my friends to help me.
All dictators do that.
I'd be different.

Something I didn't want to tell you:
What?
I like somebody.
Is he nice?
Yes! I'm miserable!

Here's the kind of job I want:
The kind where I can wear
outrageously high heels all day.

Also, here's something
I've noticed lately:
If you are very, very, quiet
time forgets you're there.

Can I be a sniper when I grow up?
No.
A hit man, then, or a scam artist?
A gold digger and a gangsta girlfriend?
Absolutely not.

Guess what is my goal?
I give up. What is your goal?
To go to the Atlantis resort
and to get a mini fridge for my room.
I'll save up.
OK.
And to be famous.
For anything in particular?
I don't know. Something good.

Psyche

I found Psyche's earring this morning:
an enormous silver hoop describing
a crescent moon, migrating dolphins,
and white feathers falling.
I knew it belonged to her, but
when I saw it on the front steps
of Grey Rock Middle School
I wanted it for myself.
I almost put it in my pocket
then thought of what she endured
in there—the pushing and shoving,
the sweaty sneakers, and the dress code.
And I considered her gentle soul
searching, searching for Eros
in smelly stairwells and cluttered rooms
where nobody ever says anything
beautiful, wise, or brave.
I thought of her dark, swinging hair
and almond eyes, her small, delicate hands
and the great tasks still before her
so I put the earring back, hoping
she would see it when she is set free at 3:05.

Public Enemy Number One

Remember when sugar was evil?
A bigger sin than salt or fat?
"Pass the white death," we'd say over coffee.
When Moira was tiny, somebody suggested
taking the kids out for ice cream,
so six of us, one baby per lap,
ended up at a ritzy ice cream parlor.
Everything was white marble and gold paint.
A crystal chandelier hung over each table.
The chairs were metal with cold little seats.
Waiters brought us the biggest, fanciest sundaes
I'd ever seen—three kinds of ice cream with hot fudge
and peppermint sticks, chocolate-covered nuts,
marshmallows, caramels, and candied cherries.
We were supposed to share them with our kids.
"Won't this give them a taste for sugar?"
I asked, holding Moira tight.
"Nothing to worry about," said the friend
whose idea this expedition was.
She had an explanation I couldn't follow
about sugar pulling enzymes into the gut.
She was a medical professional, after all
and an experienced mother of two
so I picked up my long-handled, silver spoon
and collapsed into the arms of the devil.

Change: A Story

"Where the hell am I? Somebody
tell me what's going on!"
My father leapt out of bed
wild-eyed and shouting.
Fortunately, it was foggy that morning.
"We're in London, Dad."
I pulled back the heavy hotel curtains.
"See? London fog!"
At first we thought it was jet lag
but he couldn't read the map
of the London Underground
or remember our room number
or cope with the currency.
"Look, Dad, *Fodor's* says
a pound is worth about. . . ."
He held a shilling in the wide
pillowed valley of his left palm.
"So this is the coin of the realm,"
he said, handing it back to me.
After that, my mother navigated
and I handled the money.
"When are the Inns of Court?" he asked.
"We went yesterday. Remember
all the copper beeches?"
"Have we been to Stratford?"
"No, Stratford is tomorrow."
We went to the theater every night,
and I discovered the little bistros
on each mezzanine that sold wine
and cookies at intermission.
I'd get something for the three of us

while my mother stayed with my father.
That's when I really learned to make change.
On our last night, we went to see
Arthur Miller's *The Price*
about the crash of 1929,
the year my mother and father
graduated from college.
We got box seats on the right.
I'd never been closer to the stage.
My hair was long then, and I wore
a light blue suit and pearls.
The lead walked downstage
and said his big final speech
about losing everything—
livelihood, family, even
faith in the future—right to me.
The attention was thrilling,
and I saw, in the brilliant
double-sided mirror he held,
my good luck to be young
on one side,
his last act, on the other.

To My Big Brother on the Vernal Equinox

I wonder what you would think
of me sitting at the kitchen table at four a.m.
studying Hanshan's eight-line poems.
Rain pelts the dark windows
helping me concentrate.
No wild gorges and cloud-soaked trails for me.
My Cold Mountain is here, in the quotidian.
Our lives diverged early, big brother,
but our hearts have traveled together
and sometimes I catch glimpses of you
far ahead on the path.

Staying Behind

"Exile is not for everyone. Someone has to stay behind, to receive letters and greet family members when they come back.

Edwidge Danticat
from *Brother, I'm Dying*

Your photos, once folded in tender, vein-blue
airmail tissue, now grafted to emails, reveal
the beauty of the Adriatic world—lakes
with island castles, rivers circling ancient
red-roofed cities: Europe with an Asian tang,
forests, mountains, fishing villages, wild horses.
But I get the feeling this is just background.

In the foreground are your petulant girlfriends,
all with the same porn star smiles and over-
plucked eyebrows, and when I finish reading the
letters, they keep talking—your Pavla, Vesna,
or Marija—berating the florist for
running out of yellow freesias, shrieking at
the waiter for ruining the calamari,
sulking until you buy them more jewelry.

I thought you wanted to be appreciated,
to belong deeply and cleave to your soul home,
which is not here, of course, the place you were born,
where I remain, opening and reading your letters.
Tell me, which one of us is home, which away?
What a Mobius strip the expat life is!
The idea of home an irrational surface
twisting out of sight, becoming its opposite.

Lately, you've been hinting you're ready to exit
the land of *cevapcici* sausage, lame dogs,

and tiny bathrooms. Just remember, back home
we're still raw, ambitious, soaked in immigrant grief.
Spring here is nothing but a knife to the heart,
and we're close to joy only in November,
sky reddening, air smelling of oil and iron.
All this will seem familiar at first, then strange.

Acknowledgments

Many thanks to the editors and publishers of the following publications in which these poems first appeared, some of them in slightly different form.

"August" and "Time and Matter in Hayden Hall," in *While You Were Sleeping I Dreamt a Poem: Cleveland Salon Anthology*, Sammy Greenspan, editor, Kattywompus Press, 2013.

"*Les Nympheas* at the *Orangerie*" and "Letter to My Mother: Julia Child," in *What I Knew Before I Knew: Poems from Pudding House Salon-Cleveland*, Sammy Greenspan, editor, Pudding House Publications, 2010.

"Old Flame," in *Awake at the End: A Heights Arts Poet Laureate Anthology*, John Panza and Mary Weems, editors, Bottom Dog Press, 2008.

Meredith Holmes

Meredith Holmes grew up in Moorestown, New Jersey, and has lived for many years in Cleveland Heights, Ohio. In the 1970s, she was part of the Big Mama Poetry Troupe, a feminist poetry theater group that performed nationally and published two collections of poetry. In 2004, Meredith's first book of poems, *Shubad's Crown* (Pond Road Press, 2003) was honored at "Writers and Their Friends," a celebration of books and writers produced by The Poets and Writers League of Greater Cleveland.

From 2005 to 2006, Meredith was the first poet laureate of Cleveland Heights and was invited to serve a second term from 2015 to 2016. Her poems have been published in journals such as *Flyover Country Review, Literary Mama,* and *Passager,* and in several anthologies, including Garrison Keillor's *Good Poems for Bad Times;* the Kattywompus Press collection *While You Were Sleeping I Dreamt a Poem; Awake at the End,* published by Heights Arts and Bottom Dog Press; and the forthcoming *How Higher Education Feels,* edited by Dr. Kathleen Quinlan. Meredith currently works as a freelance writer, specializing in workplace and environmental issues and women in science.

Joan Pereira

Joan Pereira was born in Buffalo, New York, in a snowstorm. As a young child, she moved to Albany, New York, where her career as an artist began. While still in grammar school, Joan won a citywide art contest which included a scholarship to the Albany Institute of History and Art. Joan's interest in art brought her to Provincetown on Cape Cod where she met the man she married. After she settled there, she studied at the Fine Arts Work Center and, for many years, with established Provincetown artists such as Bruce McKain, Philip Malicoat, Henry Hensche, Fritz Pfeiffer, Jim Forsberg, Myron Stout, and Edwin Dickinson. In addition to drawing and painting, Joan works in glass mosaics, clay, and pastels. A grant from Yale University sent her to Provence for a season of painting in the seventies. She has also painted for long periods in Peru, Bolivia and Ireland. Today, she continues to work each morning *en plein air* or in her studio.

Joan's cover painting for Meredith Holmes' book, *Familiar at First, Then Strange*, continues the theme of Holmes' title. Joan explains: "I was reading a lot of Franz Kafka when it struck me that his analysis of a village bore a striking resemblance to Provincetown, the village I live in. So I called this early morning painting of my village, 'Kafka's Village at Dawn.'"

Joan's work can be seen in Provincetown at The Provincetown Pilgrim Monument and the Provincetown Art Association and Museum; and at the Indian Museum in Anchorage, Alaska; the Bethlehem Steel Historic Museum in Bethlehem, Pennsylvania; and the San Antonio Airport in Texas.

Colophon

The title font used is Adobe Lithos Pro, designed in 1989 by Carol Twombly. The basic shapes of ancient Greek inscriptions chiseled into stone inform this typeface. Lithos is imbued with a liveliness appropriate to a wide variety of display jobs, including something that seems familiar at first, then strange.

The body text is set in Minion Pro, an Adobe Original font designed by Robert Slimbach. Inspired by classical typefaces of the late Renaissance, Minion is a highly readable typeface, combining modern sensibilities with elegance, beauty with functionality, and versatility with old-style elements.

This book was printed by Lightning Source Incorporated in the United States of America.

8/27/15

WITHDRAWN

Holmes, Meredith
811
Hol   familiar at first, then strange

	DATE DUE		
SEP 15 2015			
11/23/15			

Wellfleet Public Library
55 West Main Street
Wellfleet, MA 02667
508-349-0310
www.wellfleetlibrary.org

CPSIA information can be obtained at www.ICGtesting.com
Printed in the USA
LVOW10s2005010715

444633LV00010B/33/P

9 780971 97